T0042874

THE MAGIC WORDS

Also by Joseph Fasano

The Last Song of the World

The Swallows of Lunetto

The Dark Heart of Every Wild Thing

The Crossing

Vincent

Inheritance

Fugue for Other Hands

THE MAGIC WORDS

SIMPLE POETRY PROMPTS THAT UNLOCK THE CREATIVITY IN EVERYONE

Joseph Fasano

A TARCHERPERIGEE BOOK

tarcherperigee

an imprint of Penguin Random House LLC
penguinrandomhouse.com

Copyright © 2024 Joseph Fasano
Penguin Random House supports copyright. Copyright fuels creativity, encourages diverse voices, promotes free speech, and creates a vibrant culture. Thank you for buying an authorized edition of this book and for complying with copyright laws by not reproducing, scanning, or distributing any part of it in any form without permission. You are supporting writers and allowing Penguin Random House to continue to publish books for every reader.

TarcherPerigee with tp colophon is a registered trademark of Penguin Random House LLC

Most TarcherPerigee books are available at special quantity discounts for bulk purchase for sales promotions, premiums, fundraising, and educational needs. Special books or book excerpts also can be created to fit specific needs. For details, write SpecialMarkets@penguinrandomhouse.com.

ISBN 9780593716878
eBook ISBN 9780593716885

Library of Congress Control Number: 2023946779

Printed in the United States of America
1st Printing

Book design by Lorie Pagnozzi

While the author has made every effort to provide accurate telephone numbers, internet addresses, and other contact information at the time of publication, neither the publisher nor the author assumes any responsibility for errors or for changes that occur after publication. Further, the publisher does not have any control over and does not assume any responsibility for author or third-party websites or their content.

For all my students, who are so often my teachers

Tonight, as you walk out

into the stars, or the forest, or the city,

look up

as you must have looked

before love came,

before love went,

before ash was ash.

Look at them: the city's

mists, the winters.

And the moon's glass

you must have held

in the beginning.

That new moon

you must have touched once

in the waters,

saying *change me, change*

me, change me. All I want

is to be more of what I am.

—Joseph Fasano

CONTENTS

Introduction

Poetry is what happens when we let ourselves be. Each one of us started this journey of life with the astonishing power of an imagination, and all too often the practical concerns of daily living encroach upon that childlike wonder, that ability to trust the dreamlike images inside us, to follow those images as a child would follow a magical creature deep into an enchanted forest, unafraid of what might be there.

In my life as a writer, I am often invited to read from my novels and books of poetry throughout the world. Although I have given talks everywhere from Harvard University to backyards, from the fog of Scotland to the sunshine of California, from the hills of Granada to the small towns of the American South, it was one very special event with young children that changed my life and taught me just how necessary poetry is in the lives of people who do not think of themselves as "poets" at all.

In 2022, I was invited to speak with a class of second graders in New Jersey, to teach them about the craft and magic of poetry. To help guide their imaginations, I developed a prompt (the first prompt in this book) that could help those young people unlock the images, thoughts, and feelings inside them, without asking them to worry about how to structure a poem. The results were astonishing: seven- and eight-year-olds were writing about their identities (how they felt like "immortal jellyfish," like "wild tigers dreaming in the sunlight," like "crazy elephants eating clocks"), their worries ("What is life?" "Am I weird?" "How do people get used to other languages?"), their self-esteem ("Always I am loyal," "I am wild," "I am kind"). As poetry has always done, the prompt was unlocking our most precious natural resource: the imagination.

———————

In the late nineteenth century, archaeologists discovered a terra-cotta tablet at Nippur, in southern Mesopotamia, in modern-day Iraq. It was over four thousand years old, and it was engraved with a mysterious text. In the fray of dailiness, it was filed away with thousands of other fragments—potsherds, tablets, bones—until, in 1951, the scholar Samuel Noah Kramer rediscovered it and decided to try his hand at translating the Sumerian text inscribed on its miraculously preserved surface.

"When I first laid eyes on it," Kramer later wrote, "its most attractive feature was its state of preservation. I soon realized that I was reading a poem, divided into a number of stanzas, which celebrated beauty and love."

And what Kramer translated was truly astonishing. The poem begins with these words:

2

Bridegroom, dear to my heart,

Goodly is your beauty, honeysweet,

Lion, dear to my heart,

Goodly is your beauty, honeysweet.

This was a voice speaking from deep in the recesses of time, a voice that was using images to express the inexpressible. It was pure, elemental language. It was unadorned. And it was the exact kind of imagery those second-grade students were using over four thousand years later in a small classroom in New Jersey. "Sometimes I am a wealthy lioness," a seven-year-old student wrote, "prancing in the fields."

When I shared that student's poem on social media, the response was tremendous. Hour by hour, day by day, the news of this poetry prompt swept the nation, and then the world. Soon, thousands of people, many of whom had been struggling with language, self-expression, or overwhelming feelings, began to use the prompt and share their results: a ninety-year-old woman working through dementia with her caretaker, an autistic sixteen-year-old grappling with verbal communication, classrooms of students whose teachers had translated the prompt into Spanish, French, Turkish, German, and many other languages. Clearly, this was not just an exercise for children. Clearly, the human spirit that had written its words on that four-thousand-year-old fragment was still, even in our modern world, even in the hearts of those who would never think to call themselves "poets," very much alive.

And that is precisely the idea of this book. There are many wonderful resources for aspiring poets and many self-help books that encourage people to connect with their feelings, but the astounding response to this project convinced me that a certain kind of book was missing: a book that provides accessible poetic structures that allow people, no matter how familiar they are with the technical aspects of poetry, to let the deepest parts of themselves speak. By providing those poetic structures, I hope to create spaces where people with no knowledge of (or even interest in) those techniques can immediately achieve the expression of a poem that speaks their deepest truths. And that is what I hope for you who are reading this book. All you need to do is let your mind freely associate as it follows the prompts, and then look, just look: on the page, or on the computer screen, or on your smartphone, a truth, a shimmering truth, will be there.

How to Use This Book

The word "prompt" derives from the Latin *promere*, which means "to bring forth" or, more poetically, "to bring to light." In this book, you will find fifty-one fill-in-the-blank poetry prompts designed to bring your inner poet out into the light. The prompts encourage you (or your students, or your children, or others with whom you share them) to think in images, bypassing the conscious mind to reveal unexpected, delightful truths. They help you organize your feelings. They offer you a map with which to find the treasures waiting inside you. They let you speak directly to others, to the world, to yourself.

Just as the universe, with all its mysteries, is composed of only a limited number of elements, every poem that expresses the inexpressible is made, miraculously, of a very limited number of words. The prompts you'll find in this book ask you to fill in the blanks using only four types of words—or "parts of speech," to use the technical term—in the belief that a small number of elements can give rise to entire universes of experiences and feelings. Here is what each of these parts of speech does:

A **noun** is a word that names a person, place, or thing.

Examples: *house, jubilation, Texas, rhinoceros, apple*

An **adjective** is a word that describes something.

Examples: *red, tremendous, steady, infinite, deep*

A **verb** is an action word.

Examples: *run, enjoy, wake, console, arrange*

An **adverb** is (most often) a word that describes a verb. Think of it as indicating how something is done.

Examples: *slowly, immensely, wholly, well, radiantly*

Most often, you'll insert a new word every time you're prompted to insert one of your own. Sometimes you'll be prompted to repeat a word: when the prompt says "Noun A," for example, you'll use that same word whenever you're prompted again to insert "Noun A." These unexpected repetitions often reveal magical transformations, and they often show us new possibilities we never could have consciously imagined. This is yet another way to unlock the hidden possibilities of language, of creativity, of yourself.

———————————

Interspersed throughout these pages are examples of how people of all ages, from all walks of life, have used some of these prompts to express the joys, sorrows, and great questions of their lives. Some people have followed the prompts precisely, and some have been moved to make changes to suit their inspiration.

You'll also find "Notes from a Poet"—sentiments I've included here and there to help inspire, delight, and guide readers of all ages.

There is no right way to use this book: play, create, enjoy, and stay inspired. The most important idea within these pages is that creativity, however serious or silly, begins with experimentation, play, and risk. So treat this book as a workbook. Carry it to the beach or park, stain it with coffee or juice, dog-ear the pages, let it meet the rain and the wind. Write in it, erase it, write some more. Or keep it pristine and write your poems and notes in a separate workbook. The prompts can be used in any order, and I encourage you to use the same prompts again and again, taking note of how your responses change over time. After all, each of us can come to learn what poetry has always known: you can always start over again.

Whether you are a parent or teacher hoping to help young people express themselves, a caretaker trying to help an elder feel heard, or a busy entrepreneur with only a few moments on the subway during your morning commute, you are the coauthor of this book. I hope you can use these prompts to wake the great and ancient voice that dwells inside us all, and I hope that they encourage you to develop prompts of your own. Maybe, on some not-so-distant day, you will find you have learned from the structures of these prompts, even subconsciously. Maybe you will find that you are the creator of a new prompt, and that you have followed it and filled it with your own soul. And then—who could say otherwise—will you not have written a poem?

SELF

When we say "the self," we do not mean just one thing. We mean all the many people, creatures, and powers dwelling inside us. This prompt helps us connect to all those different forces so that they can speak.

SELF POEM (TITLE)

My name is _____.
(YOUR NAME)

Today I feel like a/an _____ _____
(ADJECTIVE A)   (NOUN A)

_____ing in the _____.
(VERB A)   (NOUN B)

Sometimes I am a/an _____.
(NOUN)

Sometimes I am a/an _____.
(NOUN)

But always I am _____.
(ADJECTIVE)

I ask the world, "_____?"
(QUESTION)

And the answer is

a/an _____ _____
(ADJECTIVE A)   (NOUN A)

_____ing in the _____.
(VERB A)   (NOUN B)

What Is Life?

My name is Marisa.

Today I feel like a wealthy lioness prancing in the fields.

Sometimes I am a fox.

Sometimes I am a wolf.

But always I am loyal.

I ask the world, "What is life?"

And the answer is

a wealthy lioness prancing in the fields.

—Marisa, New Jersey, age 7

QUESTIONS

"These days," James Baldwin once wrote, "everybody knows everything, [and] that's why so many people are lost." By that he suggests it's sometimes necessary to set aside our search for answers and to fully embrace the mysteries of the uncertain. When we follow the questions, we often find the road is even more rewarding than any destination. This prompt helps us feel that perhaps we are designed to become the questions as much as the answers. Ending a poem on a question of our own helps us hear, as if for the first time, its importance, its depth, and its many meanings.

QUESTION POEM (TITLE)

Why is the _____ _____?
       (NOUN)   (ADJECTIVE)

Why is the _____ _____?
       (NOUN)   (ADJECTIVE)

Why is the _____ _____?
       (NOUN)   (ADJECTIVE)

When I ask, I hear the song of my own

_____ voice.
   (ADJECTIVE)

And then I know the answer.

The _____ is _____,
     (NOUN)   (ADJECTIVE)

the _____ is _____,
    (NOUN)   (ADJECTIVE)

and the _____ is _____
        (NOUN)   (ADJECTIVE)

because we are meant to love

the _____ questions.
    (ADJECTIVE)

_____?
(INSERT A QUESTION OF YOUR OWN AS THE FINAL LINE.)

13

AFFIRMATION

Bertolt Brecht once wrote, "In the dark times / Will there also be singing? / Yes, there will also be singing. / About the dark times." This prompt helps us remember that there is always a way to affirm the present. Reaching back into the past, we can touch a positive memory and be transformed once again into the self we thought we lost, a self that is even more aware of how precious it is.

_____

AFFIRMATION POEM (TITLE)

Let the _____ be _____.
  (NOUN) (ADJECTIVE)

Let the _____ be _____.
  (NOUN) (ADJECTIVE)

Let every _____ inside me find its _____
  (NOUN) (NOUN)

and _____ _____, _____
  (VERB) (ADVERB) (ADVERB)

toward this world.

I have a story I have never told:

Once, when I was _____,
  (ADJECTIVE)

I looked up at the _____ and saw the _____
  (NOUN) (NOUN)

and knew I was a/an _____ made of _____.
  (NOUN A) (NOUN B)

I am still a/an _____ made of _____.
  (NOUN A) (NOUN B)

15

Affirmation

Let the fears be short.

Let the funerals be beautiful.

Let every memory inside me find its way

and walk carefully, slowly toward this world.

I have a story I have never told:

Once, when I was alone,

I looked up at the sky and saw shadows of my family

and I knew I was a girl made of angels.

I am still a girl made of angels.

—Emily, New York, age 13

Notes from a Poet

The life of a writer is a life of becoming,
day by day, a better listener—to others, to
yourself, to the world, and to the words
we have to witness them.

LOVE

Love often stuns us into silence. All we can do sometimes is sigh, shine, or even weep for joy. But often we wish to express just how much we love. Perhaps the greatest kind of love to receive is the love that helps us fully be ourselves, and if we are truly well in mind and spirit, we are able to receive this love and give it in return. This prompt helps us say to someone, "Yes, you make me what I've always hoped I was."

LOVE POEM (TITLE)

The moon is just a/an _____ without your
(NOUN)

_____.
(NOUN)

The sun is just a/an _____ without your _____.
(NOUN) (NOUN)

The wind is just a/an _____ without your _____.
(NOUN) (NOUN)

And I am just a/an _____ without your _____.
(NOUN) (NOUN)

Let me say it this way, and let it last:

The moon is the moon when you _____.
(VERB)

The sun is the sun when you _____.
(VERB)

The wind is the wind when you _____.
(VERB)

And when you _____ me, I am what I am.
(VERB)

GUILT/SHAME

The fear of being an outcast is deeply rooted in the human spirit, because in prehistoric times, being cast out of the group—into the harsh weather, into the wilderness with its fangs and claws—meant great danger. With this fear in our hearts, we carry around guilt or shame, sometimes rationally, sometimes irrationally, and are afraid to admit it, even to ourselves. This prompt helps us give words to our guilt or shame and move from the wilds of silence into the field of self-forgiveness, which is one step closer to reentering the warm embrace of the others.

GUILT/SHAME POEM (TITLE)

I have been the _____ _____
(ADJECTIVE)   (NOUN)

_____ing among the _____
(VERB)   (ADJECTIVE)

_____s in this world.
(NOUN)

I have been the silence in the _____.
(NOUN)

I have been the _____ in the _____,
(NOUN)   (NOUN)

the _____ in the _____.
(NOUN)   (NOUN)

But it is time. It is time.

_____ is knocking at my door,
(NOUN)

wearing its _____ _____
(ADJECTIVE)   (NOUN)

of _____.
(NOUN)

Life, my _____,
(NOUN)

admit it.

21

A Slow Reckoning

I have been the saintly girl

sitting among the right ways in this world.

I have been the silence in the stone.

I have been the dust in the room,

the walls in the house.

But it is time. It is time.

Truth is knocking at my door,

wearing its sharp sword of words.

Life, my desire,

admit it.

—Sara, Oregon, age 32

Notes from a Poet

If there's a story you need to hear that no
one has told, become it.

GRATITUDE

Sometimes we forget to give thanks to what helps us, moves us, or gives us life. And sometimes we forget that even experiences that seem entirely negative, such as losses, sorrows, and endings, can be hidden gifts if we can only look at them differently or wait for them to change us in ways we never expected. This prompt helps us slow down and be mindful about what something inside us wishes to thank.

GRATITUDE POEM (TITLE)

I thank the earth for its _____.
 (NOUN)

I thank the sky for its _____.
 (NOUN)

I thank the sea for its _____.
 (NOUN)

I thank the wind for its _____.
 (NOUN)

I thank the body for its _____.
 (NOUN)

I thank the beginning for its _____.
 (NOUN)

I thank the end for its _____.
 (NOUN A)

Yes, I thank even the end.

What would the beginning be

without the _____ _____
 (ADJECTIVE) (NOUN A)

of the end?

DISAPPOINTMENT

When we embark on a new task, we have already succeeded in overcoming what many do not overcome: the fear of taking a risk. D. H. Lawrence once wrote, "I never saw a wild thing / sorry for itself." This prompt helps us turn, in our disappointment, toward the natural world to see how it tries again and again without despair.

DISAPPOINTMENT POEM (TITLE)

Even the moon sometimes fails to _____.
(VERB)

I tried. I woke each day in _____
(NOUN)

and _____ed
(VERB)

and _____ed
(VERB)

and thought I was a/an _____.
(NOUN)

Now I stand here _____ in the _____,
(ADJECTIVE)   (NOUN)

and my heart is a/an _____ _____,
(ADJECTIVE)   (NOUN)

and my hands are _____ _____s.
(ADJECTIVE)   (NOUN)

Look:

the _____ _____ing
(ANIMAL)   (VERB A)

in the _____
(NOUN)

fails to _____ the _____
(VERB)   (NOUN)

but _____s
(VERB)

and _____s
(VERB)

and goes right on _____ing.
(VERB A)

27

ANGER

Anger is often thought of as a purely negative emotion, but that is only so when it is destructive. Anger, if expressed in a healthy and constructive way, can reveal itself as an ancient adaptation that allows us to distance ourselves from what is not our truth. This prompt helps us tell the world that we know how to express our anger.

ANGER POEM (TITLE)

The _____ sings peacefully
 (NOUN A)

in the _____.
 (NOUN)

But I am not the _____.
 (NOUN A)

I am the _____ _____
 (ADJECTIVE) (ANIMAL)

_____ing _____ in the _____.
 (VERB) (ADVERB) (NOUN)

And I know how to _____.
 (VERB)

Echidna

The dove sings peacefully in the early morning.

But I am not the dove.

I am the malevolent serpent

twisting quietly in the night.

And I know how to bite.

—Kimberly, Minnesota, age 25

FROM THE WRITER:

I drew inspiration from Echidna, a Greek mythological monster that is half woman and half serpent. Sometimes when I am angry I feel that I share her "hideous" and "poisonous" attributes, with the other part of me holding the purity of a dove.

Notes from a Poet

Another day, another chance to make the
mistake that will save you.

HAPPINESS

And then there are the times when we get to step out into the light. Joy is often wordless, but happiness has words. This prompt helps us express a moment of happiness, perhaps so that we can revisit it in times when we've forgotten that light.

HAPPINESS POEM (TITLE)

This is what I wanted: to be _____.
(ADJECTIVE)

Why was I _____ for so long
(ADJECTIVE)

in the _____ _____?
(ADJECTIVE)   (NOUN)

I love you, _____.
(NOUN)

I love you, _____.
(NOUN)

I love you, _____.
(NOUN)

_____, you do not scare me.
(NOUN)

Tonight I will sleep in the _____,
(NOUN)

but I will wake again _____ing
(VERB A)

in the _____.
(NOUN A)

I will wake again _____ing
(VERB A)

in the _____.
(NOUN A)

SADNESS

At the heart of creativity is the belief that our unwillingness to feel our true feelings will only result in more sorrow, and perhaps even in destructive or self-destructive behavior. When we are sad, we must enter the shadowy house of sadness and eat the dark bread, drink the sour milk, sit on the cold floor. When we have finished the feast, and only then, we can rise again and walk out into the light.

SADNESS POEM (TITLE)

I stand at the door of _____
                               (NOUN)

and am afraid to _____.
                      (VERB)

But I will _____.
                (VERB)

I go in.

I touch the _____, the _____.
                  (NOUN)   (NOUN)

I touch the _____ _____
                   (ADJECTIVE)   (NOUN)

in the _____.
          (NOUN)

This is the feast of sorrow:

the _____ and _____ on the table.
        (NOUN)   (NOUN)

What can I do but eat?

_____, I know you are waiting
     (SOMETHING YOU LOVE)

in the sunlight.

But first I must _____ in the shadows.
                      (VERB)

First I must _____ my _____.
                  (VERB)   (NOUN)

GRIEF

Grief is a natural part of life. If we mourn for someone or something deeply, we feel just how much love we had—and still have—for what we've lost. Psychologists, philosophers, and artists agree that we must feel those feelings fully so that we can move through them. This prompt helps us embrace the difficult feelings so that we can let go.

GRIEF POEM (TITLE)

I miss your smell of _____.
(NOUN)

I miss your voice like _____
(ADJECTIVE)

_____.
(NOUN)

I miss your hands like _____
(ADJECTIVE)

_____ _____ing
(NOUN)   (VERB)

in the _____.
(NOUN)

But I know that living means _____ing.
(VERB)

And I want to live. I want to _____.
(VERB)

And you, _____, I want you to be
(NAME)

the _____ _____.
(ADJECTIVE A)   (NOUN A)

Go, be the _____ _____.
(ADJECTIVE A)   (NOUN A)

Opening Day

I miss your smell of red clay.

I miss your voice like cracking of ball against bat.

I miss your hands like hard mitts softening in the catch.

But I know that living means swinging.

And I want to live. I want to try.

And you, Dad, I want you to be the roar of the crowd.

Go, be the roar of the crowd.

—Ashley, Florida, age 43

FROM THE WRITER:

My dad died six months ago. Baseball was a religion in our home. He loved to play, teach, and coach his children. I put games on in the background at home so I feel he's still in the room with me.

Notes from a Poet

A writer is someone who believes
in other people.

WORRIES

Everyone, no matter how young or old, has had sleepless nights, anxious mornings, troubled afternoons. We worry about small things (school tests, a bad hair day, a missed bus) and big things (life and death, our families, the future of the earth). Anxiety is what we feel when we have not yet connected to the real fear, the great thing we're afraid of. This prompt helps us connect to that fear so that we can move through it and heal.

WORRY POEM (TITLE)

When I wake at night in _____
(EMOTION)

and feel like a/an _____ in the _____,
(NOUN) (NOUN)

when I _____ in the morning in _____
(VERB) (EMOTION)

and feel like a/an _____ under the _____,
(NOUN) (NOUN)

when I _____ in the moonlight
(VERB)

in _____
(EMOTION)

and feel like a/an _____ above the _____,
(NOUN) (NOUN)

I think of _____
(NOUN)

and lie down in _____
(EMOTION)

and remember that the _____
(NOUN)

is _____,
(ADJECTIVE)

that the _____ is always _____,
(NOUN) (ADJECTIVE)

and that I am a/an _____ _____
(ADJECTIVE) (NOUN)

_____ing in the _____
(VERB) (NOUN)

and am free.

SILLINESS

What is life without a little silliness? Comedy, playfulness, and even outright goofiness can help us be present, be childlike, and even deal with some of the hardest trials of being alive. This prompt encourages us to embrace the inner joker, who, as Shakespeare knew, is the one who often tells the deepest truths.

SILLY POEM (TITLE)

Give me something _____.
(ADJECTIVE A)

Give me something _____.
(ADJECTIVE B)

I'll mix them in a/an _____
(NOUN THAT RHYMES WITH ADJECTIVE A)

and give you something _____.
(ADJ THAT RHYMES WITH ADJECTIVE B)

No one knows my _____.
(NOUN THAT RHYMES WITH YOUR NAME)

No one knows my _____.
(NOUN THAT RHYMES WITH "ENOUGH")

But I know I am _____,
(NAME)

and that is quite enough!

LONELINESS/ SOLITUDE

Loneliness differs from solitude in that loneliness is a feeling of isolation, separation, being without the company you need. Solitude, however, is the enjoyment of your own company, when you feel at peace with the moon, the stars, books, memories, and yourself. This prompt helps us move from the ache of loneliness to the comfort of solitude.

LONELINESS/SOLITUDE POEM (TITLE)

After _____ing all day,
(VERB)

I walk out through the _____
(NOUN)

and _____ among the _____s.
(VERB) (NOUN)

No one knows where I am.

And then I hear it:

the _____ of the _____,
(NOUN) (NOUN)

the _____ _____
(ADJECTIVE) (NOUN)

in the _____,
(NOUN)

and I am _____. I am finally _____.
(ADJECTIVE A) (ADJECTIVE A)

No one knows where I am.

And Then I Hear It

After solitude all day,

I walk out through the twilight

and stay among the shadows.

No one knows where I am.

And then I hear it:

the murmur of the children,

the sweet voices in the dark,

and I am soothed. I am finally soothed.

No one knows where I am.

—Betsy, Massachusetts, age 83

FROM THE WRITER:

I am almost eighty-four now. Long ago I dreamed of being a poet. As it turns out, I have been many things in life, but never a "real" poet. I enjoy your prompts and love reading the poems that others have shared, and every once in a while, I like to spend an hour or two seeing what might be lurking in my brain.

Notes from a Poet

Hard truths don't have to be written in beautiful ways. Sometimes a sentence has to be perfectly ugly.

FEAR

The great psychologist Carl Jung once taught us, "Where your fear is, there is your task." Fear has many purposes, and since we are often afraid of the truth, afraid of taking the great risk of becoming ourselves, we can often use the presence of fear to understand that we are very close to the place where our true lives must be waiting. If you are afraid of something, ask yourself if it is because you are encountering a great truth. This prompt helps us say yes to those truths, as scary as they might be.

FEAR POEM (TITLE)

Yes, I _____ whenever I see the _____.
          (VERB)   (NOUN A)

Yes, I _____ whenever I hear the _____.
          (VERB)   (NOUN B)

Yes, I _____ whenever I think of the _____.
          (VERB)   (NOUN C)

But not today.

Today I will wear my _____ _____
                          (ADJECTIVE)   (NOUN)

and _____ in the _____
          (VERB)   (NOUN)

where the _____s are.
                (NOUN)

_____, look at me.
   (NOUN A)

_____, hear me.
   (NOUN B)

_____, think of me.
   (NOUN C)

Yes, yes, yes, yes, yes.

THE SHADOW

The Polish poet Czesław Miłosz once wrote, "What has no shadow has no strength to live." Similarly, the American poet Galway Kinnell sang out, "Half my life belongs to the wild darkness." Across the world, throughout time, people have understood that if we deny the darker parts of ourselves, those "shadow" parts have a way of taking control of our lives. This prompt helps us enter the shadowy rooms of our lives to find the wisdom that might be waiting there. Perhaps only with that wisdom can we truly step into the light and know that we are there.

THE SHADOW POEM (TITLE)

The _____ has a shadow.
　　　　(NOUN)

The _____ lives half in darkness.
　　　　(NOUN)

My shadow walks beside me

like a/an _____ _____
　　　　　　　(ADJECTIVE)　　　　(NOUN)

still _____ from the _____
　　　(ADJECTIVE)　　　　　　　　(NOUN)

it _____ed through.
　　(VERB)

It knows where we must _____.
　　　　　　　　　　　(VERB)

Shadow, other half of me,

sometimes only _____ things know the way.
　　　　　　　(ADJECTIVE)

I'll follow you. I'll _____ with you awhile.
　　　　　　　　　(VERB)

I'm not afraid of what I'll _____ in the darkness.
　　　　　　　　　　　　　(VERB)

SELF-ACCEPTANCE

Audre Lorde once wrote, "Nothing I accept about myself can be used against me to diminish me." One of the great struggles in life is the battle with the self, and one of the truly great achievements is to accept that self completely. Only you can know all your virtues, and only you can know all your imperfections, and therefore only you can love yourself with the most meaningful love of all, the love that embraces the whole of what you are. What you are, though, is not a fixed thing; it is always changing. This prompt helps us express what it means to find our dynamic selves, embrace those selves, and move confidently into whatever is to come.

SELF-ACCEPTANCE POEM (TITLE)

The _____ cannot help being _____.
　　　　(ANIMAL)　　　　　　　　　　　　　　　(ADJECTIVE)

The _____ cannot help being _____.
　　　　(PLANT)　　　　　　　　　　　　　　　　(ADJECTIVE)

The _____ cannot help
　　　　(CELESTIAL BODY)

being _____.
　　　(ADJECTIVE)

And I cannot help being _____.
　　　　　　　　　　　　　　(NAME)

Even in my sleep, I dream of _____.
　　　　　　　　　　　　　　　　(SOMETHING YOU LIKE)

Even in my sadness, I love my _____.
　　　　　　　　　　　　　　　　(NOUN)

I swim in the rivers of my _____.
　　　　　　　　　　　　　　(NOUN)

I climb through the mountains of my _____.
　　　　　　　　　　　　　　　　　　　(NOUN)

I travel for years and years.

And on the other side

is _____, beautiful _____,
　　(YOUR NAME)　　　　　　　　　(YOUR NAME)

my _____　_____
　　　(ADJECTIVE)　　　　　　(NOUN)

_____ing in the _____.
　　(VERB)　　　　　　　　　　(NOUN)

Am I?

The fox cannot help being.

The tree cannot help being.

The stars cannot help being.

And neither can I.

Even in my sleep I am.

Even in my sadness I am.

I swim in rivers of my existence.

I climb through mountains of my being.

I travel through this world.

And at the end of it all

I am.

Name shining through the gloom, I am.

—H. Collins, Ohio, age 16

A NOTE:

A mother wrote to me to say that her sixteen-year-old autistic daughter took some creative liberties with the self-acceptance prompt, and I love what she created. Feel free to make your own changes to the prompts in this book to fit your mood, your inspiration, or your style!

Notes from a Poet

Go into the world with boldness.
Remember: that voice you heard in the
beginning, that song you were so afraid of,
that story you knew would carry you, that
was the voice you have learned to love.
Those were your truths, your magic words.
That was you.

FRIENDSHIP

The ancient Greeks had many words for the different kinds of love. *Philia* was their word for the love between friends. In some languages, such as contemporary English, we lack the words to differentiate between kinds of love. This poem helps us speak to those friends who love us, support us, and help us stay true to ourselves.

FRIENDSHIP POEM (TITLE)

You and I are _____ and _____.
(NOUN) (NOUN)

You and I are _____ing and _____ing.
(VERB) (VERB)

When I am deep in _____,
(NOUN)

you come to me like a _____ing _____.
(VERB) (NOUN)

When you are lost in _____,
(NOUN)

I go to you like a _____ing _____.
(VERB) (NOUN)

Let the world say everything is _____.
(ADJECTIVE)

I would bring you _____
(NOUN)

if you were _____.
(ADJECTIVE)

CRUSHES

Adoring someone from afar is fun, terrifying, and sometimes painful. Have you ever felt that someone you adore might not even be aware that you exist? This prompt calmly invites another person to go on a journey with you (either real or imaginary) to get to know who you are.

CRUSH POEM (TITLE)

I watch you as you look at the _____
                                        (NOUN A)

outside the _____
                    (NOUN)

and I know you wouldn't see me

even if I were _____ing in the _____,
                        (VERB)   (NOUN)

even if I were the _____ itself.
                            (NOUN A)

But I am not the _____.
                          (NOUN A)

In all my dreams, I come and sit beside you

like the _____ in your _____,
                  (NOUN)   (NOUN)

like the _____ _____,
                  (ADJECTIVE)   (NOUN)

like the _____ in the _____
                  (NOUN A)   (NOUN)

that no one hears.

But I hear me. I hear me.

We could _____. We could _____ there
                  (VERB)   (VERB)

together.

Where is the world where you can hear my _____?
                                                              (NOUN A)

59

Ripening

I watch you as you look at the lemon trees outside the window

and I know you wouldn't see me

even if I were blooming in the sunlight,

even if I were the lemon tree itself.

But I am not the lemon tree.

In all my dreams, I come and sit beside you

like the instruments in your studio,

like the warmed cup of tea,

like the lemon tree in the garden that no one hears.

But I hear me. I hear me.

We could escape. We could take root there together.

Where is the world where you can hear my lemon tree?

—Emily, Texas, age 24

Notes from a Poet

If any song in you stops singing when you're
with someone, it is not love.

BREAKUPS

Letting go can be extremely difficult, especially when our sense of self is tied up with whatever we are stepping away from. And yet something wise in us knows that true love is the continuous act of loving all the changes, all the dimensions, of another person, and receiving that same gift in return. Every loss on the way to that love is an opportunity to grow. As I once wrote in a poem, we are only as immense as what we surrender. This prompt helps us take back our lives and love ourselves for what we are, even if no one else can yet see our unique magic.

BREAKUP POEM (TITLE)

You ask me if I am _____.
(ADJECTIVE A)

But I am not _____.
(ADJECTIVE A)

I swore you were the _____ in my life.
(NOUN A)

I hoped you were the _____.
(NOUN B)

Now I walk out of this _____ _____
(ADJECTIVE)   (NOUN)

and see the _____ for the first time
(NOUN C)

and know that you are not the _____.
(NOUN C)

I am the _____,
(NOUN A)

and I am the _____,
(NOUN B)

and I am the _____.
(NOUN C)

PARTING

No matter our age, we experience feelings of separation: a child leaving for school, a parent left at the bus stop, a teenager experiencing a breakup, a middle-aged person weathering a divorce. If we don't express what we feel, and if we don't put it into some form, we can easily become overwhelmed. This prompt helps us confront and express how we feel about parting from what seems like our entire world.

_____

PARTING POEM (TITLE)

I was the _____ and you were the _____.
(NOUN A)   (NOUN B)

I was the _____ and you were the _____.
(NOUN C)   (NOUN D)

Now I watch you _____ into the _____,
(VERB A)   (NOUN E)

and though I am _____,
(ADJECTIVE)

though my heart is _____,
(ADJECTIVE)

all I want is for you to _____ in the _____.
(VERB)   (NOUN)

Once, we _____ed together in the _____.
(VERB)   (NOUN)

But now you are _____ing into the _____,
(VERB A)   (NOUN E)

and you are the _____, and I am the _____,
(NOUN A)   (NOUN B)

and you are the _____, and I am the _____.
(NOUN C)   (NOUN D)

CHANGE

At the end of his great poem "Archaic Torso of Apollo," Rainer Maria Rilke breaks out in a sudden realization: "You must change your life." Often this command comes into our minds in the most seemingly regular moments: when we are walking the dog, or staring at a sunset, or speaking with someone we've known for years. This prompt helps us listen to that voice within.

CHANGE POEM (TITLE)

I am done with being _____.
(ADJECTIVE)

I am done with _____ing in the _____.
(VERB)   (NOUN)

I am done with not _____ing _____.
(VERB)   (ADVERB)

Life, help me to _____.
(VERB)

All I want is to _____ like a/an _____
(VERB)   (NOUN A)

in the _____
(NOUN)

the way I did when I was not _____.
(ADJECTIVE A)

_____, _____
(YOUR NAME)   (ADJECTIVE)

_____, say it:
(NOUN A)

I am not _____.
(ADJECTIVE A)

Waves

I am done with being silent.

I am done with falling in the sea.

I am done with not singing loudly.

Life, help me to breathe.

All I want is to rise like a wave in the ocean

the way I did when I was not scared.

Maud, rising wave, say it:

I am not scared.

—Maud, France, age 50

Notes from a Poet

Wake today and say, "I will let every thought, every feeling, happen to me. I will not turn them away. How do I know what my life is trying to do with me?"

MISTAKES

"Freedom is not worth having," Mahatma Gandhi once reflected, "if it does not include the freedom to make mistakes." Something that is perfect is unchanging, unmoving, even without a need to speak. That sounds like the opposite of life. To be alive is to change, to move, to have a voice that tries to right wrongs, to reconcile differences, even to make ruin beautiful. This prompt helps us find the blessing in every mistake.

MISTAKE POEM (TITLE)

This is how a/an _____ _____s,
                         (NOUN)   (VERB)

by losing its _____.
               (NOUN)

This is how a/an _____ _____s,
                         (NOUN)   (VERB)

by falling in _____.
              (NOUN)

This is how a/an _____ _____s,
                         (NOUN)   (VERB)

by stumbling on _____.
                 (NOUN)

I am what I am, a/an _____ _____
                             (ADJECTIVE)   (NOUN A)

that loses, that falls, that stumbles,

and then that _____s.
                (VERB A)

Look at me. Look at my _____.
                       (NOUN)

This is how a _____ _____s.
                  (NOUN A)   (VERB A)

APOLOGY/ FORGIVENESS

So often in life, we get caught in the past because we are unable to forgive either ourselves or others. Regret is a powerful and useful emotion, but we should regret only long enough to change. Do we want one another to suffer or to be changed? Too often in our society, we're told we should want to punish instead of teach, to suffer instead of atone. The first version of this prompt can help you express an apology, and the second version can help you express forgiveness. Apology and forgiveness: two sides of the same human mystery.

APOLOGY POEM (TITLE)

I could have seen the _____ in your eyes.
(NOUN)

I could have felt the _____ in your heart.
(NOUN)

I could have heard the _____ in your voice.
(NOUN)

But I was _____. I was not
(ADJECTIVE)

the _____ _____.
(ADJECTIVE A)   (NOUN A)

Listen: there are words to say

that can change us.

Can I say them? Can I still be changed?

_____, _____, listen:
(SOMEONE'S NAME)   (NOUN)

I promise I will be the _____ _____.
(ADJECTIVE A)   (NOUN A)

_____

FORGIVENESS POEM (TITLE)

I know. I know you know

what you've done to _____.
                          (NOUN)

I know your days are _____ _____
                          (ADJECTIVE)   (NOUN)

and _____.
        (NOUN)

I know that you are lost now

in the _____.
            (NOUN)

Listen: there are words to say

that can change us.

Will you say them? Will you _____ them?
                                    (VERB)

Will you _____ them?
                (VERB)

_____,
    (SOMEONE'S NAME)

I, too, have _____ed in this one life.
                  (VERB)

Look up at the _____ _____s
                      (ADJECTIVE)   (NOUN)

in the _____.
            (NOUN)

Even the _____s get to come home again.
                (NOUN)

74

Notes from a Poet

Live every moment like the moment you
were born, when you didn't ask permission
to be you.

SPIRITUALITY

Not everyone believes in God, or gods, or other spiritual presences, but some of the most compelling spiritual poetry throughout history has been written from places of doubt, disbelief, or crisis. And of course there is great poetry written by believers, expressing their gratitude and closeness to their higher powers. This prompt can help us address, thank, or even quarrel with those higher powers.

SPIRITUALITY POEM (TITLE)

_____, you have been the _____
(GOD'S NAME)   (NOUN)

in my _____.
        (NOUN)

You have been the _____ I _____
                        (NOUN)   (VERB)

in the _____.
        (NOUN)

And now I _____ you to _____ me.
            (VERB)   (VERB)

I ask you to be the _____ that _____s
                        (NOUN)   (VERB)

me across the _____ of my life.
                (NOUN)

Do not _____ me now.
        (VERB)

Come to me as a/an _____ of _____,
                        (NOUN)   (NOUN)

a/an _____ _____.
        (ADJECTIVE)   (NOUN)

_____ me like the _____
(VERB)   (ADJECTIVE)

_____ of the _____.
(NOUN)   (NOUN)

MANTRA

Sometimes the best way to start the day is to repeat a mantra, a word or phrase that helps focus the mind on its presence and purpose. Alone, in a moment of quiet, you can address the secret, sacred thing in you that knows where it is going. Reminding yourself to trust that part of you is a healing and transformative act. There's a special kind of magic in the repetition at the end of this prompt.

MANTRA POEM (TITLE)

No one knows the _____ that
(ANIMAL A)

_____s in me.
(VERB A)

No one knows my heart is a/an _____
(ADJECTIVE)

_____
(NOUN)

I carry through the _____ toward the _____.
(NOUN) (NOUN)

No one knows the _____ I softly _____.
(NOUN) (VERB)

But I do. I do.

I will wake today and _____ my _____.
(VERB) (NOUN)

I will walk today and _____ the _____.
(VERB) (NOUN)

I will _____ until I _____ the _____.
(VERB) (VERB) (NOUN)

_____, _____,
(ANIMAL A) (VERB A)

_____, _____.
(VERB A) (VERB A)

DREAMS

There was a time when people truly listened to their dreams. Have we moved away from that? Can we trust the images that are welling up inside us, trying to guide us in their own mysterious ways? Try this prompt as soon as you wake, without pausing to think about what you're writing. Then take a look at what you've written to see what it is trying to say to you.

DREAM POEM (TITLE)

I have dreamt of a/an _____ _____.
(ADJECTIVE) (NOUN)

I have dreamt of a/an _____ing _____.
(VERB) (NOUN)

I have dreamt of a/an _____ in the _____.
(NOUN) (NOUN)

Always, in my dreams, I wish to see _____,
(SOMEONE'S NAME)

but instead I see a/an _____ in a/an
(NOUN)

_____ _____.
(ADJECTIVE) (NOUN)

Instead I wake and see the _____ _____.
(ADJECTIVE) (NOUN)

Tell me, _____, where will I find you
(SAME NAME)

in the _____ of dreams?
(NOUN)

Or am I supposed to find you in the _____?
(NOUN)

81

Heaven-side

I have dreamt of a crushed Toyota
I have dreamt of a pleading Father.
I have dreamt of Mother in the gravel.
Always, in my dreams, I wish to see the living,
but instead, I see two graves in a secluded corner.
Instead, I wake and see the empty lane.
Tell me, angels, where will I find you
in the shadows of dreams?
Or am I supposed to find you in the heart?

—Tammy, Utah

Notes from a Poet

What three words would you say to your
younger self if you could?

WISHES

The Nobel Prize–winning writer Albert Camus once wrote an essay about Sisyphus, a mythological figure who was condemned to roll a heavy rock up a hill again and again, with no apparent meaning; that was his punishment. Camus asked if everyone's life at times seems as absurd as Sisyphus's: we look around and ask what we are doing with our lives, and why. We wish to be elsewhere, or even to be someone else. And yet Camus understood that there is one greatest kind of happiness: the wish to be exactly where you are.

WISH POEM (TITLE)

If I were a/an _____, I'd wish I were a/an
(NOUN A)

_____.
(NOUN B)

If I were a/an _____, I'd wish I were a/an
(NOUN B)

_____.
(NOUN C)

If I were a/an _____, I'd wish I were a/an
(NOUN C)

_____.
(NOUN A)

Where does all the wishing end?

In a little house, where there is _____,
(NOUN)

a _____, some _____, and
(NOUN) (NOUN)

_____,
(SOMEONE'S NAME)

laying the _____ on the table.
(NOUN)

And _____, _____, sitting
(YOUR NAME) (YOUR NAME)

at that table,

_____ing,
(VERB)

wishing to be there.

85

EPIPHANIES

It's both wonderful and difficult to have a sudden, life-changing realization, because doing so often means we have to step into a new life. This prompt helps us understand that what feels like the end of everything is often just a beginning that we do not yet have words for.

EPIPHANY POEM (TITLE)

All my life I tried to be the _____
(ADJECTIVE)

_____.
(NOUN)

All my life I thought happiness was

a/an _____ _____
(ADJECTIVE)   (NOUN)

_____ing in the _____.
(VERB)   (NOUN)

All my life I was afraid to _____.
(VERB)

Now I stand before the mirror

and see the face of a/an _____
(ADJECTIVE A)

_____
(NOUN A)

that knows how to _____.
(VERB A)

_____, don't be afraid.
(YOUR NAME)

You are a/an _____ _____.
(ADJECTIVE A)   (NOUN A)

All you have to do is _____, _____,
(VERB A)   (VERB A)

_____, _____, _____.
(VERB A)   (VERB A)   (VERB A)

87

The Topiary's Great Uprising

All my life I tried to be the ornamental bush.
All my life I thought happiness was
a perfect shrub hiding in the garden.
All my life I was afraid to take up space.
Now I stand before the mirror
and see the face of a dense thicket
that knows how to grow.
Angel, don't be afraid.
You are a dense thicket.
All you have to do is grow, grow, grow, grow, grow.

—Angel, Philippines, age 27

Notes from a Poet

Try again. Try again. The human heart is
the only thing in this universe that can open
again while knowing why it closed.

MORNING

What is the first thing you reach for in the morning? If we have a moment—when the alarm clock isn't ringing, when the bus isn't waiting, when the baby isn't wailing—we can take that time to prepare ourselves for the day ahead. This prompt helps us greet the day with strength, awareness, and gratitude.

MORNING POEM (TITLE)

I hear the _____ in the _____.
          (NOUN)   (NOUN)

I smell the _____ _____ing.
            (NOUN)   (VERB)

I feel my heart _____ing like a _____.
                (VERB)   (NOUN)

Soon I will start the work of _____ing.
                             (VERB)

But first let me _____.
                 (VERB)

First let me hear my voice as it whispers,

"On the last day of the world

I would wake and _____, _____,
                 (VERB A)   (VERB A)

_____."
(VERB A)

NATURE

Nature is what we come from, and nature is what we will return to. Because of this, we often feel that a moment of contact with nature— at the beach, on a camping trip, or even just on a neighborhood stroll—can restore us in ways that nothing else can. This prompt helps us pause in the mystery of nature and be restored.

NATURE POEM (TITLE)

Look at the _____.
(NOUN)

Look at the _____.
(NOUN)

Pause with me a moment

and hear the _____ _____ing.
(NOUN) (VERB)

Here is where I'm home, among the _____.
(NOUN)

When I was lost, the _____
(NOUN A)

_____ed to me,
(VERB A)

calling me to the _____ _____.
(ADJECTIVE) (NOUN)

There I heard the song of _____.
(NOUN)

Come with me through the _____.
(NOUN)

Listen. The _____ is/are _____ing.
(NOUN A) (VERB A)

SPRING

"April is the cruellest month," wrote the great poet T. S. Eliot, reminding us that although the freshness of spring can be a delight, it can also be a challenge. Sometimes it is hard to be the blossom, to open, to try again. This prompt helps us look at ourselves and tell ourselves that it is finally time, no matter how frightened we are, to do the miraculous thing.

SPRING POEM (TITLE)

I touch the face of the _____ in the mirror.
(NOUN)

Even the trees know this:

It is time to _____.
(VERB)

Spring

I touch the face of the fear in the mirror.

Even the trees know this:

It is time to let go.

—Lori, Minnesota, age 43

Notes from a Poet

Embrace what's difficult. Who taught you that love, wonder, and learning were supposed to be easy?

SUMMER

Especially for young people, summer is an in-between time, a time of play and rest and exploration after one world has ended and before another begins. No matter where we are in life's journey, this prompt helps us remember that playfulness, helps us remember those carefree days when it seemed we had the power, among beautiful games and clear skies, to write our own stories.

SUMMER POEM (TITLE)

Summer, you are like a friend I'll never _____.
(VERB)

When everyone is _____ing, being
(VERB)

_____,
(ADJECTIVE)

you and I can _____ into the _____
(VERB)   (NOUN)

the way we did when I was just a/an _____,
(NOUN)

when life was _____,
(ADJECTIVE)

when home was not a/an _____,
(NOUN)

and all we had to do to make it _____
(ADJECTIVE)

was _____ beyond the _____
(VERB)   (NOUN)

in the _____
(NOUN)

and build our _____
(NOUN)

and listen to the _____
(NOUN)

and tell the story that begins _____.
(INSERT THREE WORDS)

99

AUTUMN

Especially in the temperate regions of the world, where the four seasons are markedly different, autumn is a time of reflection, as it calmly reminds us that everything that is born also fades away. Look at the wonderful colors of the trees, which seem to say there are beautiful truths that can be expressed only by what doesn't last forever. This prompt helps us stand among the falling things of autumn and finally give in to a difficult but transformative truth we have resisted for so long, on our way to love what ends.

AUTUMN POEM (TITLE)

I wake and hear the _____
(NOUN)

that I have _____ed.
(VERB)

Summer was a/an _____ _____
(ADJECTIVE)   (NOUN)

_____ing with my _____
(VERB)   (NOUN)

in its _____.
(NOUN)

But that is over.

All things _____. All things _____.
(VERB)   (VERB)

Today I want to _____ into the _____
(VERB)   (NOUN)

and stand there, _____ing,
(VERB)

the _____ leaves falling onto me
(ADJECTIVE)

like _____s on my _____.
(NOUN)   (NOUN)

It is time to fall into my _____.
(NOUN)

101

WINTER

Winter can mean bitter cold, icy pavements, treacherous journeys. But it can also mean cozy evenings, hot tea, long stories by a fire. What is winter if not a chance to hold someone and be held? And why can't those arms that hold us be our own? This prompt helps us feel that closeness and step out into the cold, as if for a long journey, leaving behind anything we don't need that would weigh us down as we go.

WINTER POEM (TITLE)

Winter, you have your beauty too:

your _____, your _____,
　　　　(NOUN)　　　　　　　　　(NOUN)

the _____　　_____
　　　(ADJECTIVE)　　　　　　　(NOUN)

of your _____s,
　　　　(NOUN)

your wind that moves

through the _____s
　　　　　(KIND OF TREE)

like the voice of my _____
　　　　　　　　(FAMILY MEMBER)

calling me to leave my _____ and _____.
　　　　　　　　(NOUN A)　　　　　　(VERB A)

Only in the cold

can we come close

to feeling the _____ of someone else,
　　　　　　(NOUN)

feeling the _____ of ourselves.
　　　　　(NOUN)

I will leave my _____s in the snow.
　　　　　　(NOUN)

I will find my coat and _____　_____.
　　　　　　　　　(VERB)　　　　　　(ADVERB)

I will leave my _____ and _____.
　　　　　　(NOUN A)　　　　　　(VERB A)

103

NEW YEAR

When a new year arrives, we are often encouraged or even pressured to make big resolutions—grand, life-altering announcements—but sometimes the seemingly smallest acts are the ones that really change our lives. What if all we need to do is quiet ourselves and listen more closely to something that our lives, our loved ones, or the world might be saying? This prompt helps us turn down the volume to hear what we must hear to change.

NEW YEAR POEM (TITLE)

While everyone is _____ing in the _____,
$\qquad$ (VERB) $\qquad$ (NOUN)

their hands full of _____s,
$\qquad$ (NOUN)

their eyes full of _____s,
$\qquad$ (NOUN)

I will do it differently:

I will walk out _____ through the _____
$\qquad$ (ADVERB) $\qquad$ (NOUN)

and sit alone beneath the _____
$\qquad$ (NOUN)

and wait for you, _____.
$\qquad$ (NOUN OR PERSON)

Quietly, quietly, I will wait.

And if you come, if you _____,
$\qquad$ (VERB)

if you _____ your _____,
$\qquad$ (VERB) $\qquad$ (NOUN)

I will _____.
$\qquad$ (VERB)

I will be there.

This Year I Will Be

While everyone is *doing* in the future,

their hands full of troubles,

their eyes full of fears,

I will do it differently:

I will walk out silently through the darkness

and sit alone beneath the stars

and wait for you, wisdom.

Quietly, quietly, I will wait.

And if you come, if you appear, if you whisper your truth,

I will be.

I will be there.

—Lisa, New York, age 56

Notes from a Poet

Your assignment tonight is to read a writer
someone told you not to.

TRAVEL

Travel doesn't have to mean catching a jet to a faraway country, or taking an expensive yacht to a lush island, or even renting a cabin for a long weekend in the woods. Travel can mean stepping out your door for a long walk and choosing to see the world afresh: the street you've never walked down, the park you've never rested in, the ducks you've never dared to sing to, like a glorious fool in the moonlight. This prompt helps us reflect on the places within ourselves that we find when we "travel," places we can then take with us wherever we go.

TRAVEL POEM (TITLE)

This is what the soul wants, newness:

these _____s, this _____,
       (NOUN A)   (NOUN B)

this _____,
    (NOUN C)

the sound of _____ _____ing
             (NOUN)   (VERB)

in the _____,
     (NOUN)

my own voice like a new and _____
                            (ADJECTIVE)

_____,
  (NOUN)

my own _____ like the _____
          (NOUN)   (NOUN)

I used to _____.
       (VERB)

I had to come this far to find my _____.
                           (NOUN D)

Now I think that I will never leave.

Even when I go, I'll bring them with me:

these _____s, this _____,
       (NOUN A)   (NOUN B)

this _____.
    (NOUN C)

I had to come this far to find my _____.
                           (NOUN D)

109

HOME

When we speak of home, we mean so much more than the place, the table, the broken window that looks out over the street where we once played. Home is a place we carry inside us, and it's wise for us to pause to reflect before we open our doors to just any knocking stranger. This prompt helps us speak to those who wish to step into our lives and be a part of what we call home.

HOME POEM (TITLE)

My home is not made of _____.
(NOUN)

My heart is not made of _____.
(NOUN A)

My soul is not made of _____.
(NOUN B)

No, my home is a/an _____ _____
(ADJECTIVE) (NOUN)

that no one can _____.
(VERB)

I am there whenever I am _____.
(ADJECTIVE)

I am there whenever I am _____.
(ADJECTIVE)

I am there whenever I am _____.
(ADJECTIVE)

Yes, you can enter.

But first repeat after me:

My heart is not made of _____.
(NOUN A)

My soul is not made of _____.
(NOUN B)

111

Home

My home is not made of gold.

My heart is not made of ice.

My soul is not made of plastic.

No, my home is a peaceful flower that no one can pick.

I am there whenever I am reading.

I am there whenever I am frightened.

I am there whenever I am calm.

Yes, you can enter.

But first repeat after me:

My heart is not made of ice.

My soul is not made of plastic.

—Lilly, New Jersey, age 8

Notes from a Poet

Every day of your life is a rough draft.

PARENT TO CHILD

Often, the loudest voice within a family is the voice of silence. There are so many things we don't say to one another, and even things we don't say to ourselves. Children who grow up with silence may even find, later in life, that they are not so great at communicating with themselves and others, and that they feel a vague and nameless shame about what's unspoken inside them. This prompt helps parents speak to their children, no matter how old those children are.

POEM BY A PARENT (TITLE)

_____, it took me so long to meet
(CHILD'S NAME)

the _____ inside me.
(ANIMAL)

It took me so long to let the _____ inside me go.
(ANIMAL)

Now that I can sing out like a/an _____,
(NOUN)

I hope that you can hear

the _____ you come from;
(NOUN)

I hope you know that you are not a _____.
(NOUN)

You are the _____ _____
(ADJECTIVE)   (NOUN)

_____ing in the _____.
(VERB)   (NOUN)

You are the _____ that no one can _____.
(NOUN)   (VERB)

What I mean is this: I _____ you.
(VERB)

If you were _____, I would let you _____.
(ADJECTIVE)   (VERB)

_____, I will _____ and
(CHILD'S NAME)   (VERB)

_____ and _____, until you
(VERB)   (VERB)

find your _____.
(NOUN)

115

NEWBORNS

The great poet John Keats thought of this world as a place where our souls have an opportunity to be shaped into unique, immortal beings. Perhaps immortality is hard for some of us to believe in, but the moment we see a newborn take a first breath in this world is a moment we watch a life take its part in the great mysteries. The world will never be the same as it was before this new soul arrived. And to a parent, the warmth of a child's first breath can feel like immortality enough. This prompt helps us welcome a newborn into our wondrous, difficult, and soul-shaping world.

POEM TO A NEWBORN (TITLE)

Little one, little _____,
(NOUN)

come into the light.

This world will give you _____s
(NOUN)

and _____s and _____s,
(NOUN) (NOUN)

but not yet, not yet.

Lie here on my chest in the _____.
(NOUN)

Breathe, just breathe.

Cry your voice of _____
(NOUN)

just for the joy, the joy of it.

Your _____ is the beginning of the world.
(NOUN)

117

FATHERS

Mothers carry us into this world, but sometimes father figures are also waiting at the doors of our lives to hold us, guide us, and steer us when we go astray. As ideas of masculinity change over time, fathers begin to explore different ways to love. Whether our relationships with our fathers have been complicated or not, this prompt helps us speak to our fathers and recognize the good in them, the souls that are trying hard to love in the ways they know how.

POEM TO A FATHER (TITLE)

I thought you were the _____ _____.
                              (ADJECTIVE)   (NOUN)

I thought you were the _____ing _____.
                              (VERB)   (NOUN)

Now I see you are the _____ that _____s
                            (NOUN)   (VERB)

in the _____.
            (NOUN)

Now I see you are the _____ in my _____.
                            (NOUN)   (NOUN)

_____, you are
    (WHAT YOU CALL YOUR FATHER)

the _____ing _____ that only
        (VERB)   (NOUN)

I can _____.
          (VERB)

Once, we _____ed together in/through
              (VERB)

the _____
          (NOUN)

and I did not know you were the _____.
                                      (NOUN A)

You are the _____.
                  (NOUN A)

119

MOTHERS

"I brought my whole self to you," Maya Angelou once wrote. "I am your mother." Our mothers carried us all the way from the other side of the darkness. They brought us to the shores of this world. They helped us stand and walk into the wilderness of our lives. This prompt helps us honor these guides, these workers, these givers of life.

POEM TO A MOTHER (TITLE)

You carried me through the _____
(NOUN)

toward this world

and laid my heart like a/an _____ in my hands.
(NOUN)

_____, you said, when it was time, and I did.
(VERB)

I moved through _____s and _____s.
(NOUN)   (NOUN)

I carried your _____ in my _____.
(NOUN A)   (NOUN B)

_____, before
(WHAT YOU CALL YOUR MOTHER)

you _____ed
(VERB)

were you also _____? Were you also
(ADJECTIVE)

_____ in _____?
(ADJECTIVE)   (NOUN)

Once, you _____ed beside me in the _____
(VERB)   (NOUN)

and told a story of a beautiful place of _____s.
(NOUN C)

I know now I am those _____s.
(NOUN C)

Your _____ in my _____ has led
(NOUN A)   (NOUN B)

me here.

121

In Memory

You carried me through the storm
toward this world
and laid my heart like a broken mirror
in my hands.
See, you said, when it was time, and I did.
I moved through shadows, through fog.
I carried your sorrows in my suitcase.
Mom, before you shattered
were you also joyful? Were you also
alive in love?
Once, you sat beside me in the stillness
and told a story of a beautiful place of songs.
I know now I am those songs.
Your sorrow in my suitcase has led me here.

—February Grace, Mississippi

Notes from a Poet

One of the most moving gifts I've ever received from my students is a book of all the seemingly random things I'd said while I was their teacher. They wrote these quotes in a beautiful little volume, in their wonderful handwriting, and presented it to me when our time together was coming to an end. I love that every time I pick up that book I get to think of my students, and I get to have them remind me of these little things that I, too, often need to hear.

CHILD TO TWO PARENTS

So often we find it hard to tell our feelings to the ones with whom we are closest. Our relationships with our parents—whether they are living, have passed on, or have never been in our lives—are complex, but speaking the truth is often the first step toward an even deeper and more rewarding relationships with them and with ourselves. This prompt helps people of all ages speak those truths to their makers.

POEM TO TWO PARENTS (TITLE)

_____, you are the _____
(PARENT 1)   (ADJECTIVE)

_____.
(NOUN)

_____, you are the _____
(PARENT 2)   (ADJECTIVE)

_____.
(NOUN)

Together you are the _____ _____ing
                          (NOUN)   (VERB)

in the _____.
          (NOUN)

I carry you with me the way a/an _____ carries
                                      (NOUN)

_____ in its _____.
(NOUN)   (NOUN)

In your language of _____, speak to me
                          (SEASON)

all my life.

I will be the _____ that _____s you.
                  (NOUN)   (VERB)

When you are strong, I will _____ you.
                                  (VERB)

When you are tired,

so tired,

I will be the one to _____ your _____.
                          (VERB)   (NOUN)

CO-PARENTS

The bond between two people who have created another life together is sacred, and whether those two people remain in a romantic relationship, they share the joy and the responsibility of raising and shaping a new person. Sometimes it is necessary to pause in the chaos of daily life, look into your co-parent's eyes, and say what you see there. This prompt helps us find words for that small but important act of solidarity.

POEM TO A CO-PARENT (TITLE)

I do not know why my _____ is _____.
(NOUN)   (ADJECTIVE)

I do not know why your _____ is _____.
(NOUN)   (ADJECTIVE)

You are the _____ of our
(MOTHER/FATHER)

_____,
(SON/DAUGHTER/CHILD/CHILDREN)

and in _____ eyes I see your
(HIS/HER/THEIR)

_____ _____;
(ADJECTIVE)   (NOUN)

in _____ voice I hear your
(HIS/HER/THEIR)

_____ _____.
(ADJECTIVE A)   (NOUN A)

Yes, come walk with me through the _____
(ADJECTIVE)

_____.
(NOUN)

The world is lost without your _____
(ADJECTIVE A)

_____.
(NOUN A)

127

SIBLINGS

Siblings may go in very different directions as they grow and change, but nothing breaks the deep bond of having come from the same mysterious place. No matter where your journeys lead, perhaps there was a time when you felt that you and your sibling(s) lived together on your own private island, a nation of your own, a place with a language of laughter, memories, and words that only you and your sibling(s) could speak. This prompt helps express this special connection that can always be a source of comfort, strength, and renewal.

POEM TO A SIBLING (TITLE)

If I am the _____,
         (NOUN)

you are the _____.
         (NOUN)

Even the _____ has a _____,
     (NOUN A)   (NOUN B)

and you are the _____
         (NOUN B)

of my _____,
     (NOUN A)

the _____ I hear when I am lost in _____.
   (NOUN)   (NOUN)

In this life, you will _____
         (VERB)

and I will _____,
      (VERB)

you will go to _____ and I to _____,
     (PLACE)   (PLACE)

but deep in each of us is _____
         (PLACE A)

and the _____ of _____
    (NOUN)   (PLACE A)

and the _____ing of its _____.
    (VERB)   (NOUN)

I will meet you there when you are _____.
             (ADJECTIVE)

129

GRANDPARENTS

Parents are there to guide us, hold us, and provide loving discipline. But grandparents have already done the hard work, and they love to dote, to spoil, and even to help their grandchildren bend the rules. Perhaps you have fond memories of a home, a room, a place where a grandparent made you feel loved in a unique way. This prompt helps us use all our senses to remember and honor the sacred spaces in which that lifelong bond was formed.

POEM TO A GRANDPARENT (TITLE)

The smell of _____,
(NOUN)

the taste of _____,
(NOUN)

the feel of _____—
(NOUN)

these are what I mean when I say

_____.
(WHAT YOU CALL YOUR GRANDPARENT/S)

These

and _____ and _____ and _____.
(NOUN)   (NOUN)   (NOUN)

Part of me will go on in this world,

but part of me will always be that child

_____ing in the _____
(VERB)   (NOUN)

of your _____,
(NOUN)

listening to your voice(s) like _____
(ADJECTIVE)

_____,
(NOUN)

knowing that the _____ will never end.
(NOUN)

131

BIRTHDAYS

Sometimes the best gift we can give someone cannot be bought with money. It is something that comes directly from the soul. This prompt helps us wish a happy birthday to someone special.

BIRTHDAY POEM (TITLE)

I would give you the _____.
(NOUN)

I would give you the _____.
(NOUN)

But even those are nothing

compared to what you already have:

your _____,
(NOUN)

your _____ _____,
(ADJECTIVE) (NOUN)

your _____ that _____s the world
(NOUN) (VERB)

with _____ _____.
(ADJECTIVE) (NOUN)

_____, give us all
(SOMEONE'S NAME)

your _____ another year.
(NOUN)

We Pluck Flowers from My Mother's Garden for Her Birthday

I would give you the *brahmakamalam.*

I would give you jasmines.

But even those are nothing

compared to what you already have:

your gentleness,

your warm hands,

your garden that wraps the world with silent bravery.

Amma, give us all

your wisdom another year.

—Suchita, India, age 19

Notes from a Poet

There are things you must begin without being ready. A life and a poem are two such things.

PETS

Our pets are so much more than animals running through our lives. They are our companions, our confidants, even our friends. They teach us about unconditional love, and since their lives are often brief, they teach us about loss, about handling loss with grace and gratitude. This prompt helps us appreciate time spent with our pets.

POEM TO A PET (TITLE)

They can say you aren't a/an _____.
(NOUN)

They can say you aren't a/an _____
(ADJECTIVE)

_____.
(NOUN)

But you are. You are.

_____, I named you for the _____
(PET'S NAME)   (NOUN)

that _____s
(VERB A)

forever in the _____ _____.
(ADJECTIVE A)   (NOUN A)

Today I need no one but you.

Let's go into the _____ and _____
(NOUN)   (VERB)

_____.
(ADVERB)

Let's _____ until the _____
(VERB)   (NOUN)

_____s.
(VERB)

Let's _____ forever in the _____
(VERB A)   (ADJECTIVE A)

_____.
(NOUN A)

137

TEACHERS

The greatest teachers empower us to trust ourselves, to speak with our own voices, and to love the great work of learning throughout our entire lives. We are never, ever finished learning. This prompt helps us thank a teacher for giving us those lifelong gifts.

POEM TO A TEACHER (TITLE)

What if I told you

that when I was _____
(ADJECTIVE)

I dreamt of a/an _____ in the _____,
(NOUN)   (NOUN)

a/an _____ _____?
(ADJECTIVE A)   (NOUN A)

What if I told you

you are that _____ _____?
(ADJECTIVE A)   (NOUN A)

What if I told you

that even when I _____ed as _____
(VERB)   (ADVERB)

as I could, no one heard.

But you did.

You gave me words to _____,
(VERB)

to _____ like a _____ in
(VERB A)   (NOUN)

the _____.
(NOUN)

What if I showed you what I've learned?

What if I _____ed?
(VERB A)

DEDICATIONS

Perhaps there is someone special for whom you would like to write a poem, someone who doesn't fall into any of the categories of these prompts. Sometimes we need to write something to that special person and we can't find the right words. Maybe we're trying to be too rational, to say everything in a way that "makes sense." Maybe what we need is a little magic, a little poetry, an expression of images that speak for themselves, images that have come up from our unconscious minds. This prompt helps us connect to those images and share them with those who deserve their own poems.

DEDICATION POEM (TITLE)

There are days when I am _____
(YOUR NAME)

and days when I am not.

My heart is a/an _____ _____ing
(ADJECTIVE)   (VERB)

_____ in the morning
(NOUN)

and a/an _____ _____ing
(ADJECTIVE)   (VERB)

_____ at night.
(NOUN)

If only I could _____ in the _____,
(VERB)   (NOUN)

I would be _____.
(ADJECTIVE)

If only I could let go of _____,
(NOUN)

I would be the _____ing _____.
(VERB A)   (NOUN A)

_____, this poem is for you.
(SOMEONE'S NAME)

To love you is to be the _____ing _____.
(VERB A)   (NOUN A)

141

Further Adventures in Poetry

My Magic Words

Use this page and the next to make a list of all the words you used in these prompts: your "magic words."

Journal Entry about My Magic Words

Use this page to journal about what your list of words tells you about yourself. Do you notice any patterns? Any recurring images? Any themes? Then try using the prompts again, thinking about how your mood, your mind, or your truth might change. Are there different kinds of images you'd like to explore? Different moods? Different—perhaps unexplored—parts of your soul?

Notes from Me

The best teachers help us become our own teachers, our own sages, our own guides. Use this page to write down "Notes from Me," little bits of wisdom you've developed while using this book. When you carry the book with you, you can open to these notes again and again and find inspiration in the things you've learned—things you can remind yourself of when you feel lost, overwhelmed, or bewildered. You can even cross out notes that you once thought were true but that have now, as everything in nature does, changed.

A Favorite Poem

Writing out a favorite poem by someone else helps us feel how it moves, how it works, how it sings. Use this page to write out one of your favorite poems (something you read in a book, or online, or anywhere at all).

Content and Form

As you've perhaps discovered in *The Magic Words*, every poem has both content and form, and in the very best poems, these two aspects are so harmonious that separating them might seem quite difficult or even artificial. And yet we can approach these aspects separately to learn something about how a poem works.

Content is *what* a poem is saying (for example, it might be about an experience with nature, or a friend, or sorrow). *Form* is *how* a poem says what it says (for example, the sounds it uses, the line breaks, the blank spaces on the page, the rhythms).

We can learn the most from our favorite poems by first letting all our ideas and impressions flow out of us. *Freewriting* means writing whatever comes into your mind, whatever moves through you, without worrying about sense or structure.

Use this page and the next to freewrite about the *content* of the poem you wrote out on the previous page.

_____

_____

_____

_____

_____

Use this page to freewrite about the *form* of the poem you wrote out on page 146. Even if you do not yet have a vocabulary for the art of poetic technique, this exercise will help you explore the mysteries of how a poem works.

When you have finished your freewriting exercise, use the "Glossary of Poetic Terms," on page 153, to find words for what you've discovered about your favorite poem. Then rewrite your reflections using your new poetic vocabulary. This exercise will help you develop a deeper understanding of how poems work their magic, and the next time you write a poem, you will have this craft, this magic, in your hands.

Free-Form Poetry Prompts

Now that you've worked through the fill-in prompts in this book, you can try your hand at some more open-ended ones. You can do these poetry excursions by yourself or with others to find inspiration. Do them in any order, at any time. If no words come to you, let silence come to you. Sometimes we can hear the words only when we've quieted the noise within.

I often tell my students that shaping a poem is a lot like sculpting something from clay: you can't sculpt anything if the clay is not there. You can use these excursions to "dig up the raw clay" in freewriting sessions. Then, if you feel moved to do so, you can use this material to sculpt your own poems.

- Spend some time with the moon. Look at it, let your mind drift, and try to be present with what you see and feel. Think about its steadiness, its changes. Think about what's steady and what's changing in your own life. After you've looked at the moon for as long as you'd like, use a notebook or the blank pages at the end of this book to freewrite.

- Spend some time with an animal. This could be a pet, or it could be a wild animal that you observe from afar. Watch the way it moves, the way it interacts with the world. Try to connect to that way of moving, that way of being. Imagine yourself into the world of that creature. Then use a notebook or the blank pages at the end of this book to freewrite.

- Spend some time with water. Yes, water. If you're near a pond, a lake, a river, or any other natural body of water, great. If not, try a pool. If not, go to your sink or bathtub and run the water

151

into a small bowl or container (no need to waste). Place the water in front of you and run your fingers through it, watch the way it moves, and think about this primal element. "Nothing in the world is as soft and yielding as water," wrote Lao Tzu, "yet for dissolving the hard and inflexible, nothing can surpass it." In your mind, move with the water; become its softness, its surrender, its strength; let it dissolve "the hard and inflexible" in you. Then use a notebook or the blank pages at the end of this book to freewrite.

- Spend some time in front of a mirror. Don't worry about this blemish or that bruise. Try to see yourself as you would approach a stranger, with compassion and curiosity. Don't look away. See what words come to you, and if those words do not feel true, wait until new ones arrive. Wait until you hear a voice that begins, calmly, to describe the stranger in front of you. Then use a notebook or the blank pages at the end of this book to freewrite.

- The greatest joy—and the greatest resource—for a writer is reading. Poems are made from unexpected connections, so I always encourage my students to read widely: poetry, fiction, history, philosophy, psychology, fantasy, comics, anything. If you're feeling stuck with your writing, take a passage from a favorite book and write or type it out. Then imagine you're the writer of that book and write the next paragraph. Let yourself imitate the writer's style (the word choices, the rhythm, the sentence structure). When you've written this paragraph, pick your favorite sentence and write or type it by itself on a blank page. Then begin freewriting in a notebook or the blank pages at the end of this book, finding your own style as you go.

Remember, the magic words are in you, waiting to change you, waiting to be said.

Glossary of Poetic Terms

The following is a (very incomplete) list of some of the terms that describe various techniques and devices used in poetry.

Alliteration: The repetition of the same sound at the beginning of two or more words.

> WHEN I DO COUNT THE CLOCK THAT TELLS THE TIME
> —WILLIAM SHAKESPEARE

Anaphora: The repetition of a word or group of words at the beginning of two or more phrases for emphasis.

> I HAVE A DREAM THAT ONE DAY THIS NATION WILL RISE UP. . . .
> I HAVE A DREAM THAT MY FOUR LITTLE CHILDREN WILL ONE
> DAY LIVE IN A NATION WHERE THEY WILL NOT BE JUDGED BY
> THE COLOR OF THEIR SKIN BUT BY THE CONTENT OF THEIR
> CHARACTER. I HAVE A DREAM TODAY.
> —MARTIN LUTHER KING JR.

Assonance: The repetition of vowel sounds (a, e, i, o, u) in two or more words.

> HEAR THE MELLOW WEDDING BELLS
> —EDGAR ALLAN POE

Consonance: The repetition of consonant sounds (all the other letters in the alphabet except *a, e, i, o,* and *u*) in two or more words. (*Consonance* most often describes such repetitions in the middle or at the end of words. This is different from alliteration, in which the repeated sounds occur specifically at the beginning of the words.)

TYGER TYGER, BURNING BRIGHT
—William Blake

Enjambment: The continuation of a sentence or phrase across a line break in a poem without punctuation at the end of the line. Enjambment can help a line express ambiguity, as in the example below. After we read the second line and revise our understanding of the first line, the original meaning of the first line remains in our minds. In this way, enjambment can help a poem hold two contrasting meanings at the same time. The great poet John Keats referred to this ability to hold contrasting ideas as "negative capability," and he saw it as the hallmark of the greatest poets.

WE MERELY KNEW IT WASN'T HUMAN NATURE TO LOVE

ONLY WHAT RETURNS LOVE.
—Louise Glück

Line Break: The place at which a line of a poem ends, either with or without punctuation.

IS THERE NO HOPE FOR ME? IS THERE NO WAY

THAT I MAY SIGHT AND CHECK THAT SPEEDING BARK

WHICH OUT OF SIGHT AND SOUND IS PASSING, PASSING?
—Paul Laurence Dunbar

154

Rhyme: The repeated sound of at least one full syllable at the end of two or more words, such as in *cat* and *rat*. If the sound at the end of the words is similar but not exactly the same, such as in *port* and *heart*, that's called a *near rhyme* or *slant rhyme*.

I'M NOBODY! WHO ARE YOU?

ARE YOU—NOBODY—TOO?
—EMILY DICKINSON

Rhythm: The cadences of stressed and unstressed syllables in a group of words. When studying poems and how they work, we can indicate *stressed syllables* (which we say with more emphasis) with a slash and *unstressed syllables* (which we say with less emphasis) with an X, as in the example line "I, too, am America," used below. For a more thorough explanation of rhythm in poetry, see page 156.

/ / / X / X /

I, TOO, AM A • MER • I • CA.
—LANGSTON HUGHES

Rhythm and Meter: A Note for the Advanced Reader

Prosody is the study of poetic rhythm and meter, and although it is my particular area of academic interest, it is beyond the scope of this book. This section serves as a brief guide to the basics, but if this material is too technical for your current purposes, feel free to skip it. Once again, there's no right or wrong way to use this book!

In poetry, we talk about both *rhythm* and *meter*. *Rhythm* is a more general term for any arrangement of stressed syllables (which we say with more emphasis) and unstressed syllables (which we say with less emphasis). Every piece of writing and speech has rhythm, intentional or unintentional. *Meter* refers to specific rhythmic patterns used in poetry, which we'll discuss in detail later.

The ancient Greeks developed some terms to help them think about rhythm and meter, which we have adapted for our study of rhythm in English.

An *iamb*, for instance, is an unstressed syllable (which we'll mark with an X) followed by a stressed syllable (which we'll mark with a slash). This can occur in one word, such as "alone." If you say the word "alone" out loud, you'll notice you put less emphasis on the "a" and more emphasis on the "lone." The "a" is unstressed; the "lone" is stressed.

X   /

A · LONE

Iambs can also occur across words, as in this line by Shakespeare, which uses five iambs in a row:

X   / X / X   / X / X /

THAT TIME OF YEAR THOU MAYST IN ME BEHOLD

Using five iambs in a row is called *iambic pentameter*, and it's one of the most common meters used in classic English-language poetry.

Other common units of rhythm, which we call *feet*, include . . .

Trochee: A stressed syllable followed by an unstressed syllable, such as in "weather."

/   X

wea • ther

Dactyl: A stressed syllable followed by two unstressed syllables, such as in "radiant."

/ X X

RA · DI · ANT

Anapest: Two unstressed syllables followed by a stressed syllable, such as in "unaware" (in some contexts).

X X /

UN · A · WARE

157

Spondee: Two equally stressed syllables in a row, such as in "bookmark."

/   /

BOOK • MARK

To get very, very technical, the practice of indicating stresses (/) and slacks (X) in a poem is called *scansion*. While these markings (and a few others) are sufficient for the study of nonmetrical ("free") verse—such as the poetry in this book—most books on the subject of prosody go woefully astray by attempting to use only an indication of stresses and slacks in their study of metrical verse, which uses patterns of stresses and slacks that are regular enough to give rise to what we call a *beat paradigm*. Think of this as the pulse that your body would internalize if you heard someone reciting a few lines of poetry with a very regular pattern of stresses. Once you've internalized this pulse, the poem can do many new and interesting things that play off (or counterpoint) that underlying pulse.

The art of writing poems with such pulses is called *metrical* writing, and it differs from free verse because of the presence of this beat paradigm against which to counterpoint. Note, though, that free verse has nothing to do with chaos, randomness, or even "freedom," as we usually imagine it. *Every* poem is made of form(s), just as every word, every phrase, every sentence is made of form(s). It is impossible to write *anything* without form—we just have to expand our ideas of what "form" means. Once we do so—once we think more deeply about our rhythms, our sounds, our line breaks, our word order—we see that every "free verse" poem discovers its own form(s), its own structures, and ultimately proves the greatest idea behind all art: form is freedom. In other words, in art (as in life, as in history, as in society), freedom is not formlessness; it is the state in which we move with the form that best helps us express and embody the truth as we know it.

When we study metrical writing, the best practice is to use what we call *double scansion*, which takes account of beats as well as stresses, slacks, and other phenomena. Again, this is beyond the scope of this book, but for those interested in exploring prosody in depth, I enthusiastically recommend Derek Attridge's *Poetic Rhythm: An Introduction.*

The Magic Stories

Hundreds of thousands of years ago, our ancestors must have looked up at the stars, or listened to distant thunder, or felt the heat of a rainless season, and heard, in their own hearts, stories—stories that helped them make sense of their world, helped them praise it, helped them feel connected to its grandeur.

Simply put, we need to tell, to hear, and even to be stories to be fully human.

The ancient philosopher Heraclitus once remarked, "Character is destiny." In other words, the stories of our lives unfold from who we are. The same is true of the stories crafted by writers: we have to go deeply into our characters—getting to know their souls, their hopes, their dreams—to understand what words they would say, what actions they would take, what lives they would lead.

I often tell my fiction-writing students to learn everything about their characters by asking very particular questions. What does your character eat for breakfast? What is her favorite flavor of ice cream? What dream did he have, again and again, when he was five years old?

Even if these details do not appear in your finished story, what you've learned about your character will live in the silences, just as what's unsaid in your own heart guides you, speaks wordlessly to others, and determines the shape of your life.

Above all, getting to know your character means hearing your

161

character's voice: their way of speaking, their tone, their vocabulary, their style of interacting with the world.

If you're having trouble finding the voice of a character, try using some of the prompts in *The Magic Words* to write poems in that character's voice. This will help you feel what the character feels about love, grief, happiness, relationships, and other wonders. Although these poems may not appear in your finished story, you will learn a great deal about your character by writing them, and that will help you find the character's story, voice, and destiny.

I myself have used some of the prompts in this book to imagine the voices of different characters—from historical figures to everyday people—and this has helped me continue to develop the empathy and compassion necessary for the creation of art and the living of a fulfilling life.

Maybe it would be most helpful if I give you an example:

In the great biblical story of Genesis, Cain raises his hands against his brother Abel and takes his life. This is a story that can resonate with us regardless of our beliefs. It speaks, mysteriously, to the deepest parts of ourselves, because deep down we know that we are all made of both shadows and light, goodness and trouble. In a way, each of us is both Cain and Abel.

I wanted to imagine what Abel would say to Cain if he could rise up again and speak to him. The "Forgiveness Poem" prompt (page 72) allowed me to do exactly that, and it helped me understand more about family, forgiveness, and the human heart.

Abel to Cain

I know. I know you know
what you've done to me.
I know your days are blackened ash
and briar.
I know that you are lost now
in the dust.
Listen: there are words to say
that can change us.
Will you say them? Will you live them?
Will you be them?
Brother,
I, too, have done harm in this one life.
Look up at the starlight in the darkness.
Even the dark stars get to shine awhile.
Come, then. Come home again and lie with me.
Tell me we are not what we have done.

Notes

Acknowledgments

I would like to thank the aptly named Whitman Elementary School for inviting me to chat with its students in January 2023, a visit that sparked the creation of these prompts. I would very much like to thank Lucy Seabra, the wide-eyed and openhearted young student who asked her teacher to invite me to that school, and I am grateful for that teacher, Cathy Bennett, who saw and nourished her students' hunger for poetry.

I'm grateful for all the teachers, parents, caretakers, and others—too many to name here—who have shared these prompts with their communities and helped countless people discover the craft and magic of poetry. And to the writers of all ages whose poems appear in these pages: thank you for being who you are.

Books are brought into existence by passionate, hardworking teams. I would like to thank Marian Lizzi for her vision in bringing *The Magic Words* into being, along with Lauren O'Neal and the entire team at TarcherPerigee. Your devotion to this vision is a gift to all who open this book to find that they, too, have been opened.

About the Author

Joseph Fasano is a poet, novelist, songwriter, and teacher. His books of poetry include *The Last Song of the World*, *The Crossing*, *Vincent*, *Inheritance*, and *Fugue for Other Hands*. His novels include *The Swallows of Lunetto* and *The Dark Heart of Every Wild Thing*. His debut album of original songs, *The Wind that Knows the Way*, was released in 2022.

Fasano's writing has been widely translated and anthologized, most recently in *The Forward Book of Poetry* 2022 (Faber and Faber). His honors include the *Rattle* Poetry Prize, the Cider Press Review Book Award, and the Wordview Prize from the Poetry Archive.

Fasano holds degrees in philosophy and poetry from Harvard University and Columbia University. To explore his work and his mission further, you can follow him on Twitter/X @Joseph _Fasano_, on Threads/Instagram @Joseph.Fasano, and online at josephfasano.net.